Hiking & Mountain Biking
DuPont State Forest

M000314696

Morning fog rolls in on Corn Mill Shoals Trail.

Hiking & Mountain Biking
DuPont State Forest

Scott Lynch

milestone press

almond, nc

Milestone Press, P.O. Box 158, Almond, NC 28702
www.milestonepress.com

Book design by Jim Parham

Cover photographs by Jim Parham, Mary Ellen Hammond, and
the author. Interior photographs by the author except as follows.
Jim Parham: pp.18-21, 29-30, 38, 42-44, 48, 60, 62, 68-70,
80-90, 98, 100; Billy "Monty" Montgomery: author photo.

Library of Congress Cataloging-in-Publication Data

Names: Lynch, Scott, 1973-
Title: Hiking & mountain biking DuPont State Forest / Scott Lynch.
Description: Almond, NC : Milestone Press, [2016]
Identifiers: LCCN 2016000049 | ISBN 9781889596334
(alk. paper)
Subjects: LCSH: Hiking–North Carolina–DuPont State
   Forest–Guidebooks. | Mountain biking–North Carolina–
   DuPont State Forest–Guidebooks. | DuPont State Forest (N.C.)
   –Guidebooks.
Classification: LCC GV199.42.N66 L96 2016 | DDC
796.509756–dc23
LC record available at http://lccn.loc.gov/2016000049

Printed on recycled paper in the United States of America

This book is dedicated to my best friend,
Billy "Monty" Montgomery.
Thanks for sharing so many outdoor adventures and
always making me laugh. See you on the trail!

Table of Contents

Mountain Bike Routes

Appendices

DuPont State

Trails (miles)

1. Airstrip Trail (1.0)
2. Barn Trail (0.5)
3. Big Rock Trail (0.9)
4. Boundary Trail (0.3)
5. Bridal Overlook Trail (0.5)
6. Bridal Veil Falls Road (0.6)
7. Briery Fork Trail (1.5)
8. Buck Forest Road (3.2)
9. Buck Ridge Road (0.6)
10. Buckhorn Creek Road (1.1)
11. Burnt Mountain Trail (2.2)
12. Camp Summit Road (0.5)
13. Cannon Creek Road (1.3)
14. Cart Trail (0.5)
15. Cascade Trail (1.3)
16. Cedar Rock Trail (1.5)
17. Chestnut Oak Road (0.5)
18. Conservation Road (2.6)
19. Corn Mill Shoals Trail (2.7)
20. Covered Bridge Trail (0.2)
21. Farmhouse Trail (0.6)
22. Fawn Lake Loop (0.6)
23. Fawn Lake Road (1.0)
24. Flat Rock Trail (0.5)
25. Flatwoods Trail (0.2)
26. Frank Street (0.3)
27. Grassy Creek Falls Trail (0.2)
28. Grassy Creek Trail (1.0)
29. Grassy Meadow Trail (0.8)
30. Guion Road (0.5)
31. Hickory Mountain Loop (1.5)
32. Hickory Mountain Road (0.9)
33. High Falls Trail (1.1)
34. Hilltop Trail (1.1)
35. Holly Road (1.4)
36. Hooker Creek Trail (1.1)
37. Hooker Falls Road (0.4)
38. Isaac Heath Trail (0.5)
39. Jim Branch Trail (1.3)
40. Joanna Road (4.2)
41. Lake Imaging Road (1.5)
42. Lake Julia Road (0.4)
43. Lake View Loop (0.2)
44. Laurel Ridge Trail (0.9)
45. Little River Trail (1.2)
46. Locust Trail (0.4)
47. Longside Trail (0.9)
48. Micajah Trail (1.0)
49. Mine Mountain Trail (1.4)
50. Moore Cemetery Road (0.2)
51. Nooks Trail (0.4)
52. Oak Tree Trail (0.5)
53. Pine Tree Trail (2.1)
54. Pitch Pine Trail (1.1)
55. Plantation Trail (1.2)
56. Poplar Hill Loop (1.4)
57. Poplar Trail (0.3)
58. Reasonover Creek Trail (3.7)
59. Ridgeline Trail (1.5)
60. Rifle Trail (0.5)
61. River Bend Trail (0.3)
62. Rock Quarry Road (1.3)
63. Rocky Ridge Trail (1.3)
64. Sandy Trail (0.6)
65. Scarlet Oak Trail (0.2)
66. Sheep Mountain Trail (1.6)
67. Shelter Rock Trail (0.6)
68. Shoal Creek Trail (1.0)
69. Shoals Trail (0.5)
70. Shortcut Trail (0.3)
71. Stone Mountain Trail (1.6)
72. Switchback Trail (0.6)
73. Table Rock Trail (0.9)
74. Tarklin Road (1.4)
75. Thomas Cemetery Road (1.6)
76. Three Lakes Trail (0.8)
77. Triple Falls Trail (1.1)
78. Turkey Knob Trail (3.3)
79. Twin Oaks Trail (0.9)
80. Twixt Trail (0.4)
81. White Pine Loop (0.2)
82. White Pine Road (0.5)
83. Wilkie Trail (0.4)
84. Wintergreen Falls Trail (0.5)

Trailheads

1. High Falls/ Visitor Center
2. Hooker Falls
3. Lake Imaging
4. Guion Farm
5. Corn Mill Shoals
6. Fawn Lake

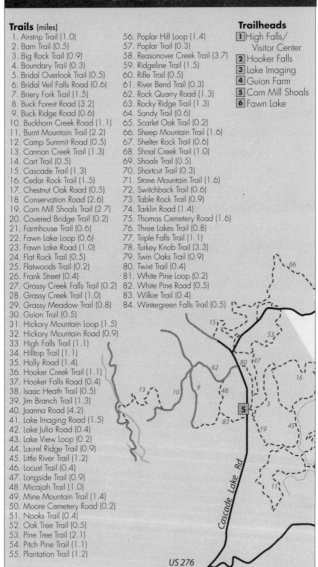

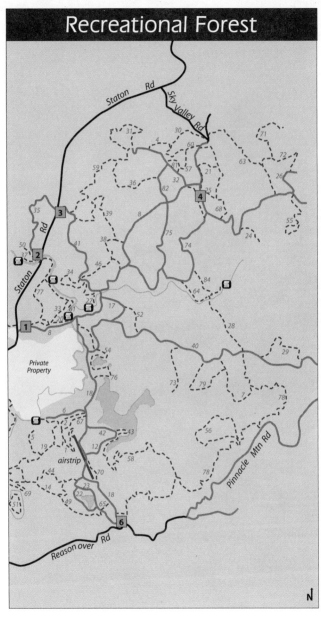

Recreational Forest

Cairns mark the route up Cedar Rock Trail.

Introduction

This book contains 27 recommended hikes and mountain bike rides in DuPont State Recreational Forest. The hikes and rides described here can take anywhere from half an hour to all day, and are suitable for most any walker, tourist, hiker, mountain biker, cyclocross rider, or trail runner. Many of the trails take the adventurer past interesting and historic places.

DuPont State Recreational Forest (commonly known as DuPont State Forest or simply DuPont) contains 10,400 pristine acres in the Blue Ridge Mountains of North Carolina. Positioned close to the border with South Carolina, it spans Transylvania and Henderson counties. Elevations in DuPont range from 2,240 to over 3,600 feet. Over 80 miles of trails traverse DuPont, providing some of the best hiking, mountain biking, horseback riding, walking, and trail running in the Carolinas.

According to the North Carolina Forest Service more than 350,000 people visited DuPont State Forest in 2012, and visitation steadily increases each year. More than 70 percent of those who come to DuPont will visit its impressive and easily accessible waterfalls. The Little River cascades over four major falls as it runs through the forest. In all, DuPont has six waterfalls within a short, easy walk from parking areas, along with five mountain lakes, including 99-acre Lake Julia.

Habitats in DuPont include upland oak forests, cove forests, granite domes, riparian areas, mountain bogs, small wildlife fields, lakes, streams, and the Little River. You'll see creatures big and small—from songbirds, peregrine falcon, bald eagles and reptiles to deer, fox and even the occasional black bear (although black bear have never been known to cause problems in DuPont).

You can hike and mountain bike here year-round, as there are few extremely hot or cold days. Temperatures range widely by season and can vary dramatically in the same day. Sunny, 60- to 70-degree days may occur anytime in winter, although 35 to 55 degrees is more typical. When it does snow, the white stuff typically doesn't stick around more than a couple of days. Summer temperatures can reach near 95 or 100 humid degrees, but that's generally only for a few weeks in August. Spring and fall in DuPont are widely considered moderate and perfect for outdoor activity, with comfortable temperatures and low humidity. Expect isolated thunderstorms in spring and summer, even on hot sunny days. These are most common in late afternoon, appear out of nowhere, and usually pass quickly.

Opportunities for outdoor recreation are just about endless. You can visit two or three dramatic waterfalls in a little over an hour, spend all day hiking the forest, or test your skills on some of the best mountain bike singletrack in the Southeast. There's something for every ability level with easy, moderate, and strenuous sections of trail.

This book contains the information you need to have a great time hiking and mountain biking in DuPont State Forest. In selecting your adventure, first assess your own fitness and skill level and look closely at the distance of the route, the elevation gain, and the trail information. If you need assistance in gearing up, you'll find plenty of excellent outdoor and bicycle shops in the area. Want to hike or ride with others? Local shops and organizations (p. 106) can be helpful in pointing you in the right direction.

Whatever you do, don't let this book sit on the shelf. Head to DuPont State Forest for memorable outdoor fun in a setting that's unforgettable.

History

The history of what we know as DuPont State Forest dates back to the late 18th century. By then, European settlers entering west-

Trail runners crossing the Little River at Corn Mill Shoals.

ern North Carolina had pushed the Cherokee Indians from the land and established farms of their own. Whiskey and lumber were important products of the DuPont area, along with copper, gold, lead and zinc.

In the early 20th century, nearly every part of what is now DuPont Forest was logged, with large water-powered sawmills in the area of Corn Mill Shoals and Bridal Veil Falls. During the 1950s DuPont Corporation began buying large tracts of land in the forest to control the supply of clean water for their chemical manufacturing process.

In the 1960s, Summit Lake (now called Lake Julia) was constructed for the purpose of establishing a children's summer camp. Camp offices, an infirmary, an airstrip, and a hanger were also built during this time. In the 1980s, the camp was sold to DuPont Corporation. By 1989, harvesting of the natural resources had all but stopped.

The DuPont State Recreational Forest was created in 1997 with a sale of over 7,500 acres to the state of North Carolina. It was a landmark event. Over the next decade nearly 3,000 additional acres were acquired through private and commercial property sales and the state's use of eminent domain. In all, DuPont State Forest comprises over 10,400 acres of permanently protected land for recreational use.

Today DuPont has a full-time staff of helpful rangers to maintain forest resources and serve its hundreds of thousands of visitors each year. Its waterfalls and verdant forest canopy appeared in the blockbuster films *The Last of the Mohicans* and *The Hunger Games*. Many hiking and mountain bike clubs consider DuPont the single best adventure spot in the Carolinas. With its rich natural and human history and the focused preservation of its pristine land, DuPont State Forest will continue to be a treasure of outdoor opportunity for generations to come.

Important Considerations

Waterfalls

The DuPont State Recreational Forest boasts six beautiful waterfalls. Hike/mountain bike routes to all of them are listed in this book.

- Bridal Veil Falls
- Grassy Creek Falls
- High Falls*
- Hooker Falls*
- Triple Falls*
- Wintergreen Falls

*These waterfalls are within a short walk from the major parking areas, and are almost always crowded.

Waterfalls are beautiful to look at, but they can be very dangerous. Every year people fall to their deaths when climbing around waterfalls. Use the following precautions at DuPont.

- Never swim, wade or play in the stream above a waterfall; it's easy to underestimate the strong flow of just a couple of inches of water
- Never climb or slide on a waterfall, and assume all rocks near it, whether wet or not, are slippery
- Supervise children closely
- Stay on established trails and enjoy the views from the official overlooks

Forest Rules

DuPont State Recreational Forest has certain rules, regulations and precautions to maintain a safe, fun, and protected outdoor experience.

- Alcohol is not permitted
- Dogs must be on a leash at all times
- Do not block any gated roads; vehicles are not allowed beyond gates unless a permit has been issued
- Fires are prohibited
- Camping is prohibited
- DuPont State Forest is a North Carolina Game Land; be aware that restricted hunting (there are safety zones) is allowed in season
- Fishing is allowed with proper state permit
- Pack out all trash; there are no trash cans in DuPont— leave no trace!
- Stay on official trails designated for your type of use

IMPORTANT DuPont State Recreational Forest has 85 trails and roads that span over 80 miles. The trails and roads are not blazed in the traditional sense, but have trail signs. So many trails and roads in the forest can be confusing. Carefully plan your route ahead of time and carry this guidebook or a map. Leave your itinerary with family and friends.

Basic Trail Rules

Hikers
- Hikers yield to horses; step off the trail
- Keep dogs under control, especially when encountering other hikers, mountain bikers or horses; horses can easily be startled by barking dogs

Bikers
- Bikers yield to all other trail users!
- DuPont trails have many slick rocks and off-camber situations. Ride within your skill level and stay in control. Slower is always better.

- Always wear a helmet
- When approaching horses, dismount your bike
- Carry a spare tube, pump, and basic tool kit

Swimming

Swimming is allowed in the lakes, streams, and near waterfalls except where prohibited as posted. Swimming is not allowed within 300 feet upstream of the top of a waterfall. Swim at your own risk— there are no lifeguards.

Exposed Rock Outcrops

Exposed outcrops are a significant feature of DuPont and can be dangerous. The Corn Mill Shoals areas of Cedar Rock, Big Rock, and Burnt Mountain—along with Stone Mountain—all have exposed rock outcrops and ridges. The tops of waterfalls can have similar topography. These steep drop-offs offer little protection from changing weather, especially storms and lightening. Be aware of your surroundings, be mindful of the conditions, and proceed with caution.

Cell Phones

While cell phones do work in many parts of the forest, they are not to be relied upon. In valleys, under thick tree canopy, and in the shadows of mountains, cell phones don't always function. When visiting DuPont, always assume your cell phone will not have a signal.

Wildlife

In DuPont, as in most natural areas, there are two major categories: the critters you likely want to see and the critters you likely don't want to see. Snakes, bear, deer, birds—they're all here.

How to see wildlife

You have a good chance of spotting wildlife on the trail, but
there are a few things you can do to increase your chances. Although
somewhat accustomed to people, the birds, deer, turkey,
squirrels, snakes, and other forest animals do their best to avoid
humans—especially a crowd of humans or a crowd of humans
making lots of noise. If you find you've been walking or riding
alone or in a small group for a while, slow down and let yourself
be quieter. You may even want to head off the trail a bit, find
a log or a big rock, and just sit silently. You'll be surprised how
quickly the forest comes alive with the sounds of animal life.

It's not uncommon to see white-tailed deer along the trail.

Another tactic is to head out on the trail either just after dawn or
just before dusk. Many animals are out and about at this time of
day to feed. Walk around quietly and see what you see.

Birding
DuPont has the distinction of being part of the North Carolina Birding Trail. That means it's a good place to see birds of all types. Year-round look for Eastern bluebird, Carolina chickadee, American goldfinch, red-tailed hawk, white-breasted nuthatch, tufted titmouse, Eastern towhee, wild turkey, downy woodpecker, and pileated woodpecker. In the warmer months you might see indigo bunting, bald eagle, ruffed grouse, broad-winged hawk, great blue heron, belted kingfisher, barred owl, scarlet tanager, black-throated blue, hooded warbler, black-and-white warbler and pine warbler, and whip-poor-will. On Lake Julia in winter you might see bufflehead and ring-necked ducks. The chances of seeing all those varieties in one outing are pretty slim—but again, go quietly early or late in the day, and who knows what might fly over.

Wildlife to look out for
Along with all the warm and fuzzy creatures in the woods are the ones you'd just as soon avoid. Usually people tend to first think, *Bears!*, and then, *Snakes!* Sure, you might be fearful of these and seek to avoid contact, but the creatures that usually cause the most problems in the forest are yellow jackets and hornets. Encountering either of these can quickly turn a peaceful walk or bike ride in the mountains into a complete panic, with people running pell-mell through the woods screaming and tearing their clothes off—it happens! Those stings can hurt like the dickens, and for anyone who is severely allergic they can be deadly. Hornets like to build their gray, football-shaped nests over water, so be especially careful around creeks and streams. Yellow jackets build their nests in the ground—sometimes right in the middle of the trail. Be cautious of insects flying in and out of quarter-sized holes in the ground. If you see a cloud of them hovering over a hole, know they're aggravated and give them a wide berth.

Hunting season
Much of DuPont Forest is a North Carolina Wildlife Game Land. During hunting season, game lands are treated differently from other public lands. Hunting is by lottery and specific days are designated for hunting deer, turkey and small game; these days fall within the state hunting seasons. Deer is typically Friday and

Saturday; turkey is typically Thursday, Friday and Saturday. In accordance with North Carolina state law, no hunting is allowed on Sundays.

Some of the more popular areas in DuPont are in hunting safety zones where no hunting is allowed. These include the waterfalls area from Hooker Falls trailhead up to the covered bridge and back to the High Falls trailhead; a small area around the Guion Farm trailhead; and the Lake Julia–Bridal Veil Falls–airstrip area. Be sure to wear blaze orange or other bright colors on hunting days when using trails outside the hunting safety zones. For current hunt dates, visit www.ncwildlife.org.

Wildflowers

If you're a wildflower enthusiast, the woods, fields, streams, waterfalls, and unique rocky mountain areas of DuPont are prime habitat for various blooms throughout the spring, summer, and fall.

Wildflower enthusiasts fall into two camps—those who like to head off on any trail at any time of the year and just see what they can see, and those who like to go in search of a particular flower, the rarer the better. If you're in the first camp, DuPont won't disappoint you. Spring bursts forth with a variety of ephemerals, those early blooming herbs seeking the sunshine on the warming forest floor before leaf-out cools things down. As we head into early summer, flame azaleas and mountain laurels brighten the hillsides, soon to be followed by rosebay rhododendron along the streams. In late summer, you might see cardinal flower growing among the boulders at the edge of streams. Before you know it, the year slips into fall and you're spotting giant Joe-Pye weed in the fields and gentians in the woods. Arm yourself with a good field guide and head off on a trail.

If you're in the second camp, there are some flowers in DuPont you won't want to miss. The white pine woods so common to DuPont are great places to see pink lady's slippers, and if you head up the slopes of Mine Mountain in May you might spot the rarer yellow lady's slipper. Head over to the spray cliffs beside the bigger waterfalls and you'll see the diminutive blooms of cave alumroot dancing in the breeze in July or take a closer look around the granite dome of Cedar Rock to spot Appalachian rock pink in mid-summer. Along the forest edges you might spy a yellow fringed orchid.

A yellow lady's slipper blooms on Mine Mountain in May.

Planning Your Trip

What to Expect

Many of the attractions at DuPont State Forest, particularly the waterfalls, are just a short walk from the major parking areas, and you'll almost always encounter crowds, park rangers, and volunteers. However, if you plan on hiking out beyond these popular areas, it's a good idea to carry basic backcountry hiking provisions. The following gear will go a long way toward keeping you safe and comfortable.

Hikers

To Carry
- Day-hiking pack with waterproof pack cover
- Trekking poles
- Properly fitted hiking footwear
- Spare pair of socks
- Carabiner on pack for strapping shoes (there are wet river/creek crossings in DuPont)
- Water container (hydration bladder or bottle)
- 2 to 3 liters of water per person
- Emergency way to purify water (tablets or filter)
- Small pocket knife
- First aid kit
- Personal hygiene items and medications
- Thermal safety blanket
- 3 ways to make emergency fire (e.g. waterproof matches, lighter, flint striker, magnesium block, etc.) and tinder

- Food and snacks
- Bag for trash
- Headlamp
- Emergency whistle
- Compass (and know how to use it)
- 550-style small tie-cord
- Small roll of duct tape
- Sunscreen
- Lip balm
- Insect repellent (if season requires)
- Way to tell time (wristwatch or phone),and know general sunset time
- Identification
- Waterproof bag or case for any electronic devices
- Provide itinerary to family/friends
- Car keys
- *Hiking & Mountain Biking DuPont State Forest*

To Wear
- Hat for sun protection
- Sunglasses with neck cord
- Bandanna
- Quick-dry clothing (no cotton)
- Season-specific layering clothing
- Rain shell

Mountain Bikers add

- Helmet
- Cycling gloves
- Spare tube(s)
- Tire pump
- Tire levers
- Tire patch/boot
- Tire pressure gauge
- Multi-tool/repair kit

Getting to DuPont & the Trailheads

It's easy to get to DuPont State Forest from metropolitan areas of western North Carolina and Upstate South Carolina. These directions will get you to the official DuPont visitor center below, open daily from 9 am to 5 pm.

Aleen Steinberg Visitor Center
1400 Staton Road
Cedar Mountain, NC 28718
828-877-6527
GPS 35.191519, -82.622235

From Brevard/Pisgah Forest, NC
1. Drive east on US 64 for 3.7 miles to Penrose.
2. Turn right on Crab Creek Road for 4.3 miles.
3. Turn right on DuPont Road, which changes to Staton Road, for 4 miles.
4. Turn left on Buck Forest Road into the gravel visitor center parking area.

From Hendersonville, NC
1. Drive south on S. Church Street.
2. Turn right on Kanuga Road and drive 3.8 miles until it changes to Crab Creek Road.
3. Continue on Crab Creek Road 7.2 miles.
4. Turn left on DuPont Road (which changes its name to Staton Road) and continue 4 miles.
5. Turn left on Buck Forest Road into the gravel visitor center parking area.

From Asheville, NC

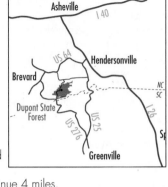

1. Take I-26 east (toward Hendersonville) for approximately 18 miles.
2. Take exit 44 to Rugby Road and drive 6 miles.
3. Turn right (west) on NC 64 and drive 7.8 miles.
4. Turn left on Crab Creek Road and drive 4.3 miles.
5. Turn right on DuPont Road (which changes its name to Staton Road) and continue 4 miles.
6. Turn left on Buck Forest Road into the gravel visitor center parking area.

From Greenville, SC

1. Drive north on US 276, passing through the towns of Travelers Rest, Marietta, and Cleveland.
2. Approximately 5.5 miles past Cleveland at the intersection of US 276 and SC 11, turn right on US 276 toward Caesars Head.
3. Drive on US 276 11.8 miles up and over Caesars Head, crossing the SC-NC state line.
4. Continue on US 276 for 1.6 miles.
5. Turn right on Cascade Lake Road (a fire department is located at this intersection).
6. Continue on Cascade Lake Road for approximately 1 mile and enter the greater DuPont State Forest area. Drive for a total of 2.5 miles.
7. Turn right on Staton Road and continue 1.5 miles.
8. Turn right on Buck Forest Road into the gravel visitor center parking area.

Directions to the Trailheads

Six major parking areas serve as trailheads for DuPont State Forest. Most of the hikes and mountain bike rides in this guidebook begin at one of these trailheads. All six have ample parking and some have toilets (although the toilet might be portable or pit-style). The trailheads below are listed east to west and in clockwise order.

Directions are given from the visitor center.

Fawn Lake Access
GPS 35.161009, -82.604136

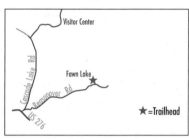

1. From the visitor center parking lot turn left on Staton Road and drive for 1.5 miles.
2. Turn left on Cascade Lake Road and drive 2.4 miles.
3. Turn left on Reasonover Road and drive 2.9 miles.
4. Fawn Lake parking area is on the left.

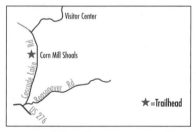

Corn Mill Shoals Access
GPS 35.172836, -82.638794

1. From the visitor center parking lot, turn left on Staton Road and drive for 1.5 miles.
2. Turn left and continue 0.7 mile on Cascade Lake Road.
3. Corn Mill Shoals parking area is on the right.

High Falls Access/Visitor Center
GPS 35.191519, -82.622235

Note This trailhead is also the starting point for directions to other trailheads.

At the far end of the parking area you'll find signs for

- Bridal Veil Falls
- Covered Bridge
- Triple Falls
- Lake Dense
- Grassy Creek Falls
- High Falls
- Lake Julia

Hooker Falls Access
GPS 35.203171, -82.619078

1. From the visitor center parking lot, turn right on Staton Road and drive for 0.9 mile.
2. Hooker Falls parking area is on the left.
3. There are lower and upper parking areas, separated by portable toilets.

Lake Imaging Access
GPS 35.209138, -82.615337

1. From the visitor center parking lot, turn right on Staton Road and drive for 1.4 miles.
2. Lake Imaging parking area is on the right.

Guion Farm Access
GPS 35.211837, -82.587943

1. From the visitor center parking lot, turn right on Staton Road and drive for 3.3 miles.
2. Turn right on Sky Valley Road; after it turns to gravel (within 0.8 mile), continue 1.5 miles on Sky Valley Road.

3. Guion Farm parking area is on the right.

Trail signs are found at all road and trail intersections.

Navigating DuPont

With all of DuPont's 84 trails and roads, it's easy to get confused by the number of pathways and intersections. The routes described in this book were chosen based on distance, difficulty, and ease of trail navigation. As you explore DuPont, carry this guidebook with you and double-check all trail intersections and turns. **Hiking routes are arranged from easiest to most strenuous.** Most of these routes are suitable for mountain biking as well (see p. 82).

Route maps accompany the description of each hike or ride. Each map shows the described route as a dashed blue line. All other roads and trails are shown in black or gray.

Route Map Legend	
▪▪▪	Route
---	other trail
▬	paved road
—	dirt road
🌊	waterfall
TH	trailhead
P	parking

High Falls invites meditation and reflection.

DuPont State Forest

Hike Routes

Hooker Falls

Hooker Falls cascades into the Little River.

Distance	0.8 mile, round trip
Difficulty	Easy
Location	West-central DuPont, off Staton Road
Time	20 minutes
Crowds	Heavy traffic, especially on weekends
Trailhead	Hooker Falls

	Route Directions
1	There are lower and upper parking lots. **From the lower parking area** begin at the end of the parking lot and to the left. There is signage for Hooker Falls Road/Holly Road. Walk down Hooker Falls Road toward the bridge. **From the upper parking lot** begin your hike by walking down the gravel pathway toward the information kiosk/bridge area.
2	To continue toward Hooker Falls, do not cross the bridge over the Little River. If walking from the lower parking area, continue straight past the bridge. If walking from the upper parking area, turn right before the bridge.

3	Continue down the wide gravel-and-dirt trail, which is mostly flat.
4	After 0.25 mile, reach the falls overlook and viewing platform.
5	Trail descends steeply for 300 ft, reaching the river level.
6	Turn left at the bottom of the hill for the best views of Hooker Falls.
7	Return to the parking areas the same way you came.

met Dave
5-25-21

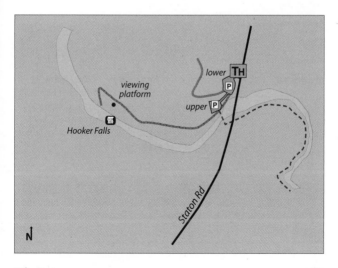

Jim Creek

Jim Creek on Flat Rock Trail.

Distance	1 mile, round trip
Difficulty	Easy
Location	East DuPont
Time	30 minutes
Crowds	Almost none
Trailhead	Flat Rock From Guion Farm parking, drive southeast on Sky Valley Road for 0.9 mile; the Flat Rock trailhead is on the right. There is pulloff parking approximately 250 ft before and 300 ft after the trailhead on the right; each spot has enough room for 3 to 4 vehicles.

Route Directions

1	From the pulloff, walk to the trailhead. Signs mark Flat Rock Trail/Sky Valley Road.

2	Begin hiking on Flat Rock Trail, heading immediately southeast into the hardwood and pine forest.
3	After 300 ft, the trail begins to descend gently into the hardwood valley.
4	At 0.4 mile, you'll begin to hear cascading water off to your left. The foliage changes to lush rhododendron.
5	Arrive at Jim Creek at 0.5 mile. This is a great spot to relax and have a look around. There are several tributary trails that wander around and even cross the creek, which is easily forded (unless after heavy rains). This trail and Jim Creek are little known; you are almost guaranteed a quiet and private hike.
6	Return to the parking area the same way you came.

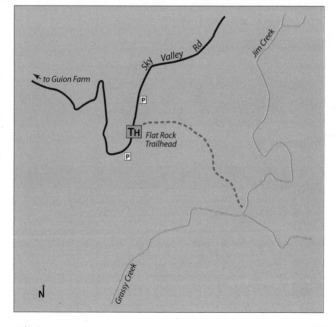

High Falls on the Little River stands 132 ft high.

Distance	1 mile, round trip
Difficulty	Easy, but with a steep climb from High Falls on return
Location	West-central DuPont, off Staton Road
Time	45 minutes
Crowds	Heavy, especially on weekends
Trailhead	High Falls/Visitor Center

Route Directions	
1	Begin your hike at the far end of the parking lot, next to the gate. Note signs for High Falls/Buck Forest Road.
2	The trail is covered in small, white, pebbled gravel as it gently descends into the valley.
3	After 0.1 mile, cross a 50-ft bridge over the creek.
4	Trail winds through S-curves, ascending slightly.

5	After 0.2 mile, come to Triple Falls trailhead intersection and trail signs; continue straight on.
6	At nearly 0.3 mile, white gravel ends. Come to an open area where three trails meet. Pay attention here and bear right, following signs for High Falls Trail.
7	After 200 ft, pass Covered Bridge Trail. Continue straight.
8	Begin descending toward High Falls. You will begin to hear the falls off to your right.
9	After another 300 ft, High Falls Trail makes a hard right and descends steeply for the next 0.1 mile.
10	After descending a steep hill, come to a split-rail fence to your right. This is the viewing and picture spot for High Falls, and is the turnaround point for this hike. The wooden steps to the left go up to a covered picnic area.
11	Return to the parking area the same way you came; it's a steep climb out of the High Falls area.

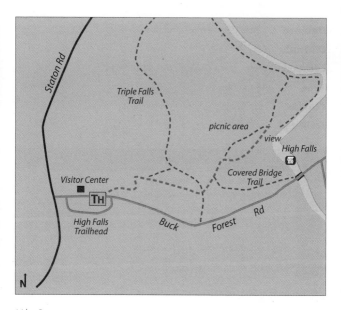

Covered Bridge

Covered Bridge at the top of High Falls.

Distance	1 mile, round trip
Difficulty	Easy
Location	West-central DuPont, off Staton Road
Time	45 minutes
Crowds	Heavy, especially on weekends
Trailhead	High Falls/Visitor Center

	Route Directions
1	Begin your hike at the end of the parking lot, to the left next to the metal gate. Note the signs for High Falls/Buck Forest Road.
2	The trail is covered in small, white, pebbled gravel, and gently descends into the valley.
3	After 300 ft, cross the 50-ft bridge over the creek.
4	Trail winds through S-curves, ascending slightly.

5	After 0.2 mile, come to Triple Falls trailhead intersection and trail signs; continue straight on.
6	At nearly 0.3 mile, white gravel ends. Come to open area where three trails meet. Pay attention here and bear right, following signs for High Falls Trail.
7	Ascend the hill for approximately 200 ft and turn right on Covered Bridge Trail.
8	On Covered Bridge Trail, go up a short hill and then it's a 0.2-mile-long downhill.
9	At 0.5 mile turn left on Buck Forest Road and arrive at the covered bridge. This is a great place for pictures of the bridge and the Little River/top of High Falls.
10	**Return options** You can either return the way you came on the trails or turn around and walk 0.5 mile back on Buck Forest Road, ending your hike at the High Falls/Visitor Center parking area. The distance is the same.

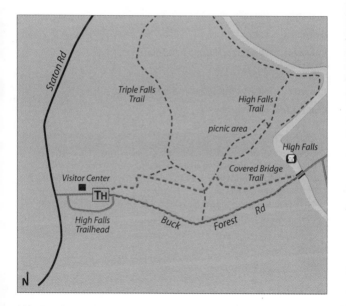

Triple Falls

Triple Falls in late summer.

Distance	0.8 mile, round trip
Difficulty	Easy
Location	West-central DuPont, off Staton Road
Time	45 minutes
Crowds	Heavy, especially on weekends
Trailhead	Hooker Falls

	Route Directions
1	**From the lower parking area** begin at the far end of the parking lot and to the left, following signs for Hooker Falls Road/Holly Road. Walk down Hooker Falls Road toward the bridge. **From the upper parking lot** begin by walking down the gravel pathway toward the information kiosk/bridge area.
2	Cross the bridge over the Little River, which officially begins the Triple Falls Trail.
3	After 150 ft the trail goes under Staton Road.

4	At 0.1 mile the trail begins to curve to the right, following the Little River to your left, and climbs gently to the Triple Falls trail-level viewing area. You'll find several spots to view this impressive waterfall.
5	At 0.3 mile, arrive at wooden stairs that descend steeply to waterfall and Little River level.
6	Return to the parking areas the way you came.

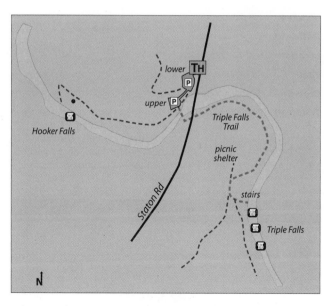

Plantation Trail

Plantation Trail strikes out through a pine forest.

Distance	1.6 miles, round trip
Difficulty	Easy
Location	East DuPont
Time	45 minutes
Crowds	Almost none
Trailhead	Plantation Trail · From Guion Farm parking, drive southeast on Sky Valley Road for 1.7 miles, cross over the bridge, and Plantation Trailhead is on the right. Park by safely pulling off the road, but do not block the trailhead.

Route Directions	
1	From the pulloff, walk to the trailhead. Signs indicate Plantation Trail/Sky Valley Road.
2	Begin hiking on Plantation Trail. The wide, flat trail begins by traversing a mostly pine forest.

3	At 0.5 mile, come to the trail's loop intersection. Bear right and head down into a lusher valley. Descend for nearly 0.3 mile, dropping 100 ft in elevation.
4	Come to the bottom of the valley at 0.8 mile and begin a steep climb; in 0.1 mile you'll gain the entire 100 ft you just lost.
5	At nearly 1.1 miles you'll return to the trail's loop intersection (same location as in route direction #3).
6	Continue mostly flat walking for 0.5 mile, back to the trailhead where you began.

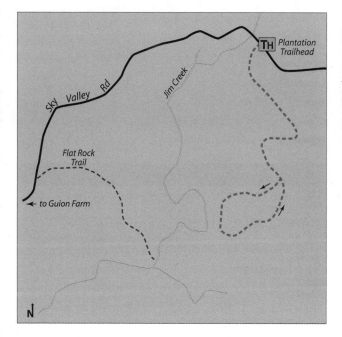

7

Grassy Creek Falls

A view of Grassy Creek Falls from the top.

Distance	2.5 miles, round trip
Difficulty	Easy
Location	Central DuPont
Time	1.5 hours
Crowds	Light to moderate
Trailhead	High Falls/Visitor Center

Route Directions	
1	Begin at the end of the parking lot by going around the gate and walking down gravel Buck Forest Road.
2	At 0.1 mile, begin a moderate 0.2-mile climb.
3	Reach the covered bridge and Little River at 0.5 mile.
4	Continue 250 ft past the covered bridge and bear left on Buck Forest Road.
5	At 0.7 mile, begin a moderate climb that lasts nearly 0.2 mile.

6	Cross a wooden bridge over Grassy Creek at 1.1 miles. Walk 100 ft and turn left on Lake Imaging Road, which begins a moderate ascent.
7	Walk 300 ft and turn left on Grassy Creek Falls Trail.
8	Continue another 650 ft on the trail to Grassy Creek Falls. Caution: the last 200 ft descends over uneven rocks and the top of the falls can be slippery.
9	Return to the parking area the same way you came.

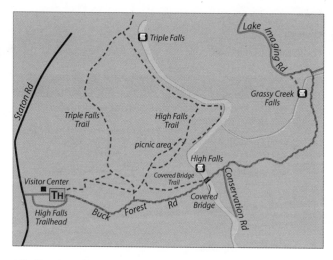

Winftergreen Falls

Wintergreen Falls drops into a nice swimming hole.

Distance	3.1 miles, round trip
Difficulty	Easy
Location	Central DuPont
Time	1.5 hours
Crowds	Light
Trailhead	Guion Farm

Route Directions	
1	At the left (southwest) side of the gravel parking lot, head south through a grassy field on an unnamed path.
2	Continue through the field for approximately 0.2 mile to an intersection. Bear right on Tarklin Branch Road.
3	At 0.6 mile, Tarklin Branch Road begins a gentle descent into a valley.
4	At slightly over 1.0 mile, bear left on Wintergreen Falls Trail.
5	At 1.4 miles at the intersection with Sandy Trail, bear left to continue on Wintergreen Falls Trail.

| 6 | At a little past 1.5 miles, arrive at 20-ft Wintergreen Falls, the most secluded waterfall in the DuPont State Forest. If you are cautious, its large boulders allow a relatively safe scramble to different vantage points of the falls. |
| 7 | Return to the parking area the same way you came. |

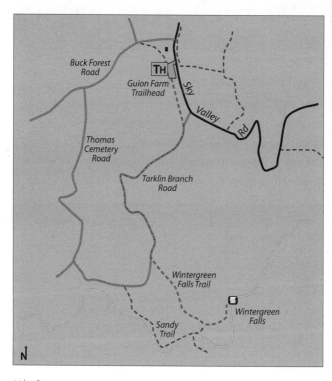

A cyclist takes a break at tiny, peaceful Lake Alford.

Distance	3.5-mile loop
Difficulty	Easy to moderate
Location	West-central DuPont, off Staton Road
Time	2+ hours to enjoy the lakes
Crowds	Heavy around covered bridge, light to moderate elsewhere
Trailhead	High Falls/Visitor Center

	Route Directions
1	Begin at the end of the parking lot by going around the metal gate and walking down gravel Buck Forest Road.
2	At 0.1 mile, begin a moderate 0.2-mile climb.
3	Reach the covered bridge over Little River at 0.5 mile.
4	Continue 250 ft past the covered bridge and turn right on Conservation Road.
5	Continue on Conservation Road for 400 ft ; turn sharp left on Pitch Pine Trail.
6	Pitch Pine Trail immediately begins a 0.2-mile climb, gaining over 100 ft.

7	At 1.1 miles cross over Joanna Road, continuing on Pitch Pine Trail, which begins its descent into the Lake Dense area.
8	At 1.3 miles arrive at secluded Lake Dense, with a covered picnic area and dock on the northwest side of the lake—a great place for lunch or just a rest.
9	Continue around the lake and at 1.5 miles turn left on Three Lakes Trail, which reenters the woods at 1.6 miles.
10	Reach the 100-ft-wide Lake Alford at 1.8 miles. A short trail connects to the lake, with a small dock and bench.
11	After Lake Alford, turn left at the trail sign to continue on Three Lakes Trail.
12	At 2.0 miles reach 99-acre Lake Julia, the largest lake in DuPont.
13	At 2.2 miles turn right on gravel Conservation Road. **Optional** For better views of Lake Julia, turn left on Conservation Road for 800 to 1000 ft.
14	Climb a moderate, 0.1-mile-long hill on Conservation Road at 2.5 miles.
15	After walking nearly 0.8 mile on Conservation Road, at 3.0 miles turn left on Buck Forest Road, crossing the covered bridge again.
16	Continue on Buck Forest Road for 0.5 mile, reaching the High Falls/Visitor Center parking area to end your hike.

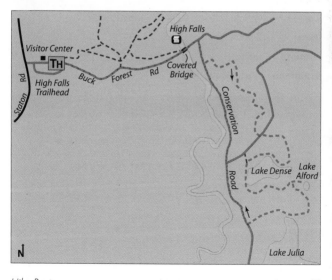

Thomas Cemetery

Entrance sign to Thomas Cemetery in DuPont State Forest.

Distance	3.4-mile loop
Difficulty	Easy to moderate
Location	Central DuPont, off Buck Forest Road
Time	2 hours
Crowds	Light
Trailhead	Guion Farm

	Route Directions
1	At the right (northwest) side of the gravel parking lot, follow the sign reading "To Hickory Mtn Rd/ To Tarklin Branch Road." Begin your hike by heading northeast, in the direction of Hickory Mountain Road. You're following an unnamed path that cuts across a grassy field, with picnic area to your right.
2	Continue for nearly 0.2 mile and turn left on Buck Forest Road. From this point, the route begins a gentle descent that continues for 1.4 miles.
3	At 0.4 mile, turn left on Thomas Cemetery Road.
4	Come to the intersection at 1.3 miles with Tarklin Branch Road on the left. Continue straight.

5	Reach the bottom of the valley at Dry Branch Creek at 1.6 miles. Trail begins easy climb.
6	At 1.9 miles, reach Thomas Cemetery on the left. This is a great place to stop, look around, and take pictures. The cemetery dates to the mid-19th century and has unique character; be respectful of the cemetery as you explore it.
7	Continuing on Thomas Cemetery Road, at 2.0 miles turn right on Buck Forest Road.
8	Continue on Buck Forest Road for 1.2 miles, climbing gently out of the valley. At 3.2 miles, turn right on the grassy field path (same location as in route directions #1 and #2).
9	Walk 0.2 mile to the Guion Farm trailhead where you began your hike.

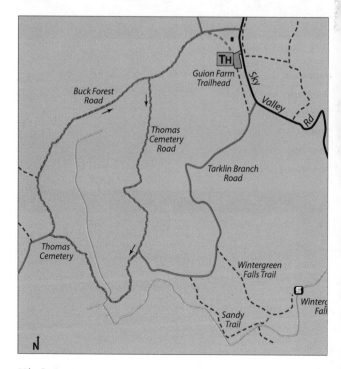

Bridal Veil Falls via Conservation Road

Bridal Veil Falls after heavy rains.

Distance	4 miles, round trip
Difficulty	Moderate
Location	South DuPont
Time	2.5 hours
Crowds	Light
Trailhead	Fawn Lake

Route Directions	
1	Begin your hike at the top of the parking lot by going around the gate.
2	Turn right on the gravel road following sign to Reasonover Creek Trail, and walk down the hill.
3	After 0.1 mile, bear left on gravel Conservation Road.
4	Road crosses over Fawn Lake Creek at 0.5 mile.
5	At 0.6 mile, bear right on Shortcut Trail, which immediately begins a 0.2-mile moderate climb.

6	Shortcut Trail parallels Airstrip Trail (an old asphalt airstrip in the middle of DuPont) at 0.8 mile.
7	At 1.0 mile continue straight, rejoining Conservation Road.
8	Begin 0.4-mile-long moderate downhill. Near the bottom of this hill, you'll begin to hear Bridal Veil Falls, though you're still over a half-mile from the waterfall.
9	At 1.5 miles, turn left on Bridal Veil Falls Road.
10	Continue down Bridal Veil Falls Road for approximately 0.5 mile, ending at Bridal Veil Falls. There is a small overlook to the right or you may venture, with caution, closer to the falls on the rocks. There are many good places to take pictures.
11	Return to the parking area the way you came.

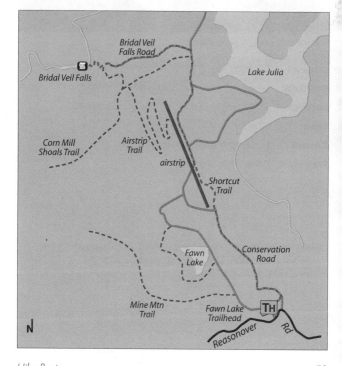

Bridal Veil Falls via Corn Mill Shoals

Bridal Veil Falls on the Little River.

Distance   5.4 miles, round trip

Difficulty   Moderate, with a technical water crossing

Location   South-central DuPont, off Cascade Lake Road

Time   3 hours

Crowds   Heavy, particularly on weekends

Trailhead   Corn Mill Shoals

Caution This hike has a wet river crossing; there is no bridge. Trekking poles, a spare pair of socks, and a way to attach footwear to your pack are recommended. The Little River may not be passable after heavy rains.

A more challenging route to Bridal Veil Falls

	Route Directions
1	Begin by crossing Cascade Lake Road and onto Corn Mill Shoals Trail.
2	After 150 ft go around the gate; come to an intersection with Longside Trail. Continue straight on, curving slightly to the right.
3	After 0.1 mile come to an intersection with Big Rock Trail. Continue straight on, curving to the right.
4	Trail begins moderate descent into a valley, then levels for 0.3 mile.
5	At 0.7 mile, come to first intersection with Burnt Mountain Trail. Continue straight, curving slightly to the right.
6	After 250 ft, come to a V-intersection with Little River Trail. Take the right path to continue on Corn Mill Shoals Trail.
7	After another 0.2 mile come to a second V-intersection with Burnt Mountain Trail. This junction can be confusing; take the trail to the left and descend into Little River valley.
8	Just past the 1.0-mile point arrive at the Little River. **Stop, evaluate water level and speed, use extreme caution, and cross the river.** The rocky riverbed is very slick and you'll find the best traction is to wear your socks with no shoes.
9	After crossing, the trail turns into traditional narrow singletrack, slowly climbing out of the creek valley.
10	After 0.2 mile, come to an intersection with Shoals Trail. Continue straight on, with the trail curving to left.
11	Trail moderately ascends to top of ridge; there are many rocks here.
12	At 1.6 miles, come to V-intersection with Laurel Ridge Trail. Take the trail to the left to continue on the Corn Mill Shoals.
13	Trail begins a descent into the valley. **Caution** Much of this descent is on rocks and water flows down these rocks almost all the time; they can be very slick.
14	Slightly past 2.0 miles come to grassy open area under powerlines. Pass the intersection with Bridal Overlook Trail and continue straight (the overlook views are in winter only).
15	At 2.1 miles, 150 yards past grassy open area, come to V-intersection with Shelter Rock Trail. Continue to the left.
16	After 0.2 mile you will begin to hear Bridal Veil Falls and see gravel Bridal Veil Falls Road below, off to your right.

Mountain bikers crossing the Little River on Corn Mill Shoals Trail.

17	At the intersection with Bridal Veil Falls Road at 2.5 miles, continue straight. Bridal Veil Falls comes into view.
18	There is a small overlook to the right, or you may venture closer to the falls. Use caution on the rocks. There are many places to take great pictures here.
19	Return to the parking area the same way you came.

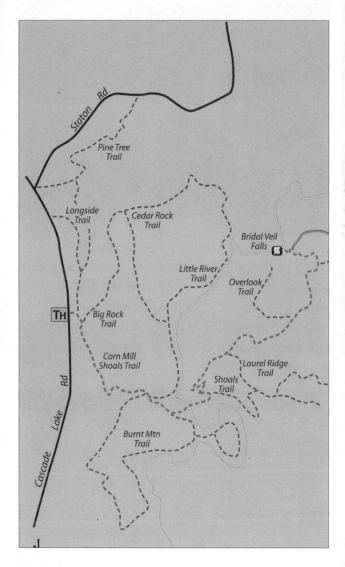

Burnt Mountain

A hiker and her "best friend" on the way to Burnt Mountain.

Distance	4.5-mile loop
Difficulty	Strenuous
Location	South DuPont, off Cascade Lake Road
Time	2.5 hours
Crowds	Moderate
Trailhead	Corn Mill Shoals

	Route Directions
1	Begin by crossing Cascade Lake Road, a wide trail with signs for Corn Mill Shoals Road/Cascade Lake Road.
2	After 150 ft, walk around the gate; come to an intersection with Longside Trail. Continue straight on, curving slightly to the right.
3	After 0.1 mile come to an intersection with Big Rock Trail. Continue straight on, curving to the right.
4	Trail begins moderate descent into a valley, then levels for 0.3 mile.

5	At 0.7 mile, turn right on Burnt Mountain Trail; the trail then climbs, steeply at times, gaining over 320 ft over the next 0.6 mile, Burnt Mountain Trail has many rock features on both sides of the path. **Caution** Water seeps from many of the rocks; they can be very slick.
6	Begin 0.6-mile descent at 1.4 miles.
7	By 2.5 miles the winding Little River will come into view below. The next 600 ft offer several excellent vantage points for pictures.
8	At 2.7 miles, turn right on Nooks Trail. The Little River is again visible as this charming trail winds around a knoll. **Variation** You can cut out 0.6 mile of this hike by bypassing Nooks Trail and continuing straight on Burnt Mountain Trail.
9	At 2.8 miles, bear right to begin the small loop of Nooks Trail.
10	Rejoin the first part of the Nooks Trail at 3.2 miles by turning right.
11	At 3.3 miles, turn right to continue on Burnt Mountain Trail.
12	Turn left on Corn Mill Shoals Trail at 3.5 miles. **Optional** Turn right at Corn Mill Shoals Trail, and walk 0.1 mile to the Little River.
13	Hike 1.0 mile to Corn Mill Shoals Trailhead to end your hike.

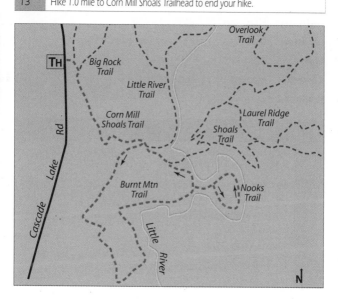

14

Cedar Rock

Bikers on the final assent to the top of Cedar Rock.

Distance	4.5-mile loop
Difficulty	Strenuous
Location	South-central DuPont, off Cascade Lake Road
Time	2.5 hours
Crowds	Moderate; busiest on weekends
Trailhead	Corn Mill Shoals

Route Directions	
1	Begin by crossing Cascade Lake Road, a wide trail with signs to Corn Mill Shoals Road/Cascade Lake Road.
2	After 150 ft, walk around the gate and come to an intersection with Longside Trail. Continue straight and then curve slightly to the right.
3	After 0.1 mile, come to an intersection with Big Rock Trail. Continue straight, curving to the right.
4	Trail descends into a valley, then levels for 0.3 mile.
5	At 0.7 mile, come to an intersection with Burnt Mountain Trail. Continue straight, curving slightly to the right.

6	After 250 ft, come to a V-intersection; take the left path to begin Little River Trail, which is mostly flat and generally parallels its river namesake for its entire 1.1 miles.
7	Cross over Tom Creek on a log bridge at 1.0 mile.
8	Come to the first intersection with Cedar Rock Trail at 1.2 miles. Don't turn here, but continue straight on Little River Trail.
9	At 1.8 miles, bear left on Cedar Rock Trail and immediately begin a 0.8-mile climb, gaining over 410 ft. Much of this traverses granite rock with many views of the surrounding mountains. Trail cairns guide you on the trail over the rocks.
10	Reach Cedar Rock Trail summit (over 3,050 ft elevation) at 2.6 miles, with outstanding northwest views. At the intersection with Big Rock Trail, continue straight on Cedar Rock Trail.
11	Begin 0.6-mile downhill back to Little River Valley.
12	At 3.2 miles, turn right on Little River Trail.
13	Continue straight on Corn Mill Shoals Trail at 3.8 miles.
14	Walk 0.7 mile to Corn Mill Shoals trailhead to end your hike where you began.

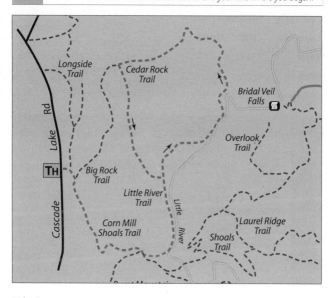

15

Lake Julia via Reasonover Creek Trail

Lake Julia.

Distance	5.3-mile loop
Difficulty	Strenuous
Location	Central DuPont
Time	3 hours
Crowds	Light
Trailhead	Fawn Lake

Caution This hike includes a rock crossing of Reasonover Creek. Trekking poles are recommended for additional stability when crossing the creek.

	Route Directions
1	Begin at the top of the parking lot by going around the gate.
2	Turn right on the gravel road, following signs for Reasonover Creek Trail, and walk down the hill.
3	After 0.1 mile, come to gravel Conservation Road. Cross the road and continue straight, following Reasonover Creek Trail.
4	Continue descending for 0.3 mile into a lush valley.
5	At 0.4 mile after crossing the creek, the trail begins a mile-long climb, sometimes strenuous, gaining over 300 ft.

6	At 1.7 miles, begin a 1.1-mile moderate descent into Reasonover Creek/Lake Julia valley.
7	Reach Reasonover Creek at 2.9 miles. Cross with caution on large, slick rocks.
8	The trail begins to parallel Lake Julia off to your right.
9	At 3.2 miles, arrive at Lake Julia, a beautiful place to relax and enjoy a snack or lunch. Enjoy the surrounding views of the largest lake in DuPont.
10	Continue onto Lake Julia Road at 3.6 miles.
11	At 3.9 miles, turn left on Conservation Road, and begin tough 0.2-mile climb.
12	At 4.2 miles, begin paralleling the old asphalt airstrip in the middle of DuPont State Forest.
13	At 4.4 miles, begin Shortcut Trail, which descends steeply.
14	Bear left (straight) on Conservation Road at 4.6 miles.
15	At 5.2 miles turn right, heading uphill toward Fawn Lake parking.
16	Arrive at Fawn Lake parking area at 5.3 miles to end your hike.

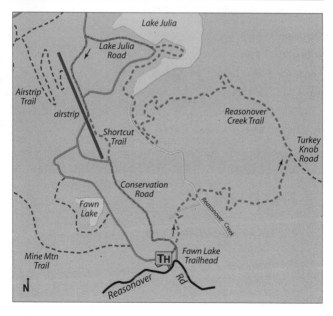

Sheep Mountain

On the Sheep Mountain loop: Cascade Trail

Distance	6-mile loop
Difficulty	Strenuous
Location	West DuPont, off Staton Road
Time	3.5 hours
Crowds	Almost none
Trailhead	High Falls/Visitor Center

Route Directions	
1	Begin your hike at the High Falls/Visitor Center parking area by walking back toward Staton Road.
2	At Staton Road, turn right and walk 350 ft.
3	Turn left at the Sheep Mountain trailhead. The Sheep Mountain Trail immediately begins a 1-mile moderate climb through a hardwood forest, gaining 240 ft.
4	At 1.5 miles, turn right on Cascade Trail. The entire 0.5-mile section of this trail is flat to gently rolling.

5	Turn left on Pine Tree Trail at 2.0 miles. Pine Tree Trail immediately begins a steep, 0.4-mile climb; this is the steepest climb of the entire hike.
6	At 2.8 miles, begin paralleling Staton Road.
7	Cross Staton Road at 2.9 miles, continuing on Pine Tree Trail.
8	At 3.3 miles, begin descending into a lush rhododendron valley.
9	At 4.1 miles, cross Staton Road, continuing on Pine Tree Trail.
10	Bear right on Sheep Mountain Trail at 4.5 miles. You are now at the same spot as route direction #4.
11	Continue on Sheep Mountain Trail for 1.4 miles, ending at Staton Road.
12	Turn right on Staton Road, walk 350 ft., and turn left into High Falls/Visitor Center parking area to end your hike.

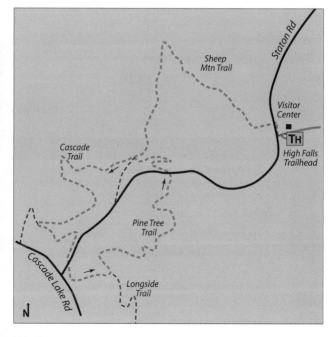

Hickory Mountain

Family hikers on the Hooker Creek Trail.

Distance	6-mile loop
Difficulty	Strenuous
Location	Northernmost hike in DuPont
Time	3 hours
Crowds	Light
Trailhead	Guion Farm

Route Directions	
1	At the right (northwest) side of the gravel parking lot, begin by heading north-east, following signs to Hickory Mountain Road on an unnamed path that cuts across a grassy field, with picnic area to your right.
2	Continue for nearly 0.2 mile, then turn left on Buck Forest Road.
3	At 0.5 mile, turn right on White Pine Road, an old roadbed.
4	Bear left on Hooker Creek Trail at 0.8 mile. The trail gently descends into a valley, losing 200 ft over the next 0.6 mile.
5	At 1.4 miles the trail begins to climb, steeply at times, gaining 500 ft over the next 1.0 mile.

6	At 1.8 miles, turn right on Ridgeline Trail.
7	At 2.0 miles, come to Hickory Mountain area. Here there are two directions for the Hickory Mountain Loop Trail and Hickory Mountain Road; turn left on the Hickory Mountain Loop Trail. The steepest climbing of the entire hike is over the next 0.4 mile, gaining over 260 ft.
8	Reach the trail summit and begin descending Hickory Mountain at 2.5 miles. Continue the descent for the next 1.8 miles.
9	At 3.0 miles, the trail begins to follow the edge of a large grassy field.
10	Arrive back at Hickory Mountain area at 3.1 miles (same location as route direction #7). Turn left on Hickory Mountain Road. The road continues around the edge of the grassy field and enters the woods at 3.2 miles.
11	At 3.4 miles, turn left on Boundary Trail.
12	At 3.8 miles turn right on Guion Trail, walk 400 ft, and turn left on Rifle Trail.
13	At 4.2 miles turn right on gravel Sky Valley Road, walk 200 ft, and take a sharp left on Shoal Creek Trail, entering a lusher valley and generally paralleling Shoal Creek to the left.
14	At 5.0 miles, turn right on Flatwoods Trail.
15	Arrive at Sky Valley Road at 5.3 miles and cross the road to the parking area to end your hike where you began it.

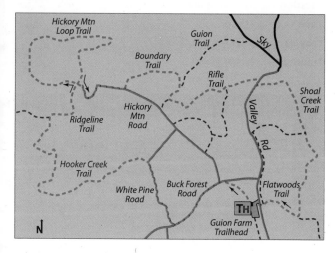

The Outer Limits

Heading up the granite path on Wilkie Trail.

Distance	7.2 miles, round trip
Difficulty	Strenuous
Location	Extreme west DuPont on mostly unknown trails
Time	3.5 hours
Crowds	Almost none
Trailhead	Corn Mill Shoals

	Route Directions
1	Begin at the Corn Mill Shoals parking area by walking toward Cascade Lake Road.
2	At Cascade Lake Road turn right. Walk 200 ft and bear right on Wilkie Trail. The trail almost immediately begins a moderate climb all the way to its end, with a couple of steep sections where you may have to watch your step in a few places.
3	At 0.4 mile, turn left on Micajah Trail. After a short reprieve the trail begins a tough 0.2- mile climb to Buck Ridge Road area.

4	Continue by bearing right on Buck Ridge Road at 0.8 mile. This is an easy trail with one small climb toward its end. The ridge offers good views of the surrounding mountains in winter.
5	At 1.5 miles, turn left on Buckhorn Creek Road for a rewarding descent into Buckhorn Valley.
6	It's a short hop across Buckhorn Creek at 2.0 miles.
7	At 2.3 miles, turn right on Cannon Creek Trail. This trail climbs for 0.4 mile before dropping into the Cannon Creek/Rich Mountain area.
8	Cross Cannon Creek at 3.3 miles and begin generally paralleling Rich Mountain Road.
9	At 3.6 miles the trail terminates at Rich Mountain Road.
10	Turn around and return to the parking area the way you came.

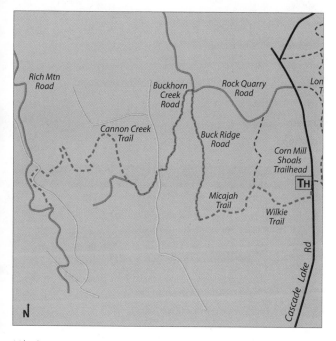

Mine Mountain with Fawn Lake

Swim dock and gazebo on Fawn Lake.

Distance	5.3-mile loop
Difficulty	Strenuous
Location	South-central DuPont, off Reasonover Road
Time	3.5 hours
Crowds	Light
Trailhead	Fawn Lake

Route Directions	
1	Begin at the top of the parking lot by going around the gate.
2	Turn left on the gravel road, following signs to Fawn Lake Road, and walk up the hill; it's a 0.5-mile climb, gaining over 250 ft.
3	After 800 ft, turn left on Mine Mountain Trail. The trail continues to climb, steeply at times, for the next 0.4 mile to over 3,060 ft elevation.
4	At 1.0 mile, come to an intersection with Cart Trail. Continue (trail immediately curves sharply right) on Mine Mountain Trail.
5	At 1.4 miles, turn left on Laurel Ridge Trail.

6	At 1.8 miles, trail begins a gentle, 0.6-mile descent into valley.
7	Turn left on Shoals Trail at 2.4 miles.
8	At 2.6 miles, bear right on Corn Mill Shoals Trail. **Optional** Bear left to reach Corn Mill Shoals on Little River in 0.2 mile.
9	Trail ascends moderately to top of ridge, with many rocks on the way.
10	Come to a V-intersection at 3.0 miles. Bear right on Laurel Ridge Trail.
11	At 3.2 miles, turn right on Cart Trail. This begins the hike's steepest climb, gaining over 200 ft in less than 0.25 mile.
12	Turn left on Mine Mountain Trail at 3.7 miles (same location as route direction #4). This begins a 1.1-mile descent back into the Fawn Lake valley.
13	At 4.1 miles, reach the intersection with Laurel Ridge Trail. Continue straight on Mine Mountain Trail.
14	Turn right on Fawn Lake Road at 4.3 miles.
15	At 4.4 miles come to an intersection with Fawn Lake Loop Trail. Continue straight on Fawn Lake Road (Fawn Lake Loop Trail is not recommended; the 0.6-mile trail navigates the west side of Fawn Lake in dense trees and does not offer many views of the lake).
16	Begin crossing Fawn Lake dam, with excellent views at 4.5 miles.
17	Continue on Fawn Lake Road for another 0.6 miles and end your hike where you began.

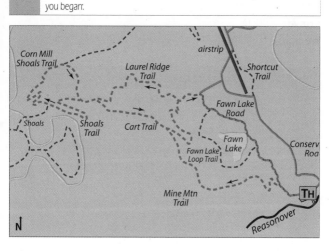

Stone Mountain

Vista from the top of Stone Mountain.

Distance	5.4 mile loop
Difficulty	Strenuous
Location	Northeast DuPont
Time	3 hours
Crowds	Light
Trailhead	Guion Farm

Route Directions	
1	Begin your hike by exiting the Guion Farm parking area. Turn left on gravel Sky Valley Road and gently descend into the valley for 0.75 mile.
2	Bear right on Old CCC Road.
3	At 0.8 mile turn right on Rocky Ridge Trail. This trail begins a steep climb away from the road; the climb continues, often steeply at times, for the next 1.8 miles and gains over 1,000 ft in elevation.
4	Turn left on Stone Mountain Trail at 1.6 miles.
5	The ascent of Stone Mountain has different topography than the rest of the route. By 1.8 miles, the trail becomes very rocky with small, unstable rocks.

6	At 2.3 miles, the trail opens to a field of tall grass. In warmer months the grass can be 6 to 10 ft high, but the trail is cut through the grass.
7	At 2.4 miles the climb becomes very steep—almost a scramble up the last 50 vertical feet to the summit of Stone Mountain.
8	Reach the Stone Mountain summit at 2.5 miles. At 3,600 ft it offers impressive panoramic views of DuPont State Forest. There is a lot to explore here; it's over 700 ft wide with many tributary paths to different vantage points and unique rock features. This is a great place to relax, have a snack or lunch, and enjoy the view. It's almost always very windy at the top, so bring a wind or rain shell.
9	After your summit fun, begin your return by heading back down Stone Mountain Trail. **Caution** There are many steep sections here with uneven footing.
10	At 3.4 miles turn left on Rocky Ridge Trail.
11	Turn right on gravel Sky Valley Road at 3.8 miles.
12	Continue on Sky Valley Road for 1.5 miles, reaching the Guion Farm parking area where you began your hike.

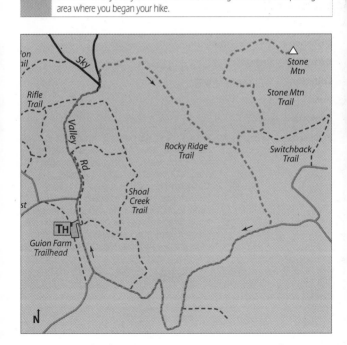

Bridge over Briery Fork Creek.

Distance	8.4 miles, round trip
Difficulty	Strenuous
Location	Southeast DuPont
Time	4 hours
Crowds	Light
Trailhead	Turkey Knob From Fawn Lake parking, drive east on Reasonover Road for 1.1 miles until the road ends. Bear left on gravel Pinnacle Mountain Road and drive 1.4 miles. **Caution** This road is rutted and rocky. Low-clearance vehicles could have difficulty, especially after heavy rains. Turkey Knob Road trailhead is on the left, indicated by a gate. You can pull off on the side of Pinnacle Mountain Road for parking.

Route Directions
1   Begin your hike on Turkey Knob Road by going around the gate.
2   Almost immediately bear right on Turkey Knob Trail.

3	Begin descending. This downhill lasts for over 1.4 miles.
4	At nearly 0.5 mile, cross a creek. By this point, you've reached a valley thick with rhododendron.
5	At 1.2 miles, turn left on Briery Fork Trail.
6	Cross Briery Fork Creek at 1.4 miles; begin a modest climb for the next 0.4 mile.
7	At 2.0 miles, turn left on Twin Oaks Trail and climb slowly for nearly a mile to a mixed-hardwood, drier part of the forest.
8	At 3.0 miles, turn left on gravel Joanna Road and climb for the next 0.25 mile.
9	Turn left on Table Rock Trail; this trail has beautiful wildflowers in the warmer months.
10	At 4.2 miles arrive at the summit and the end of Table Rock Trail. In winter there are views to Lake Julia. This is a great place to take a break and have lunch or a snack.
11	Return to the parking area the same way you came.

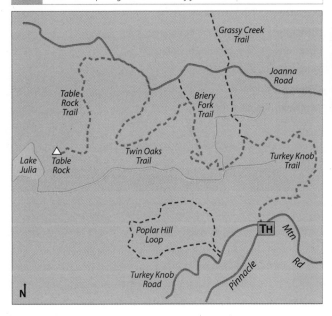

This classic sign welcomes visitors at the High Falls trailhead.

Distance   15.8-mile giant loop

Difficulty   Strenuous, due to distance only

Location   Covers most areas of DuPont

Time   6 to 8 hours

Crowds   Light

Trailhead   Hooker Falls

Caution Start early! Take 3 liters of water minimum for each hiker, along with a way to filter or purify water and sufficient energy food for all-day activity.

	Route Directions
1	From Hooker Falls upper parking area, begin by walking up the gravel road on the north side, parallel to the parking area (Moore Cemetery Road).
2	After 400 ft bear right on Holly Road.
3	At 1.1 miles come to Staton Road. Cross the road and walk 150 ft to the right to the Lake Imaging parking area.
4	On the north side of the Lake Imaging parking area, walk down Lake Imaging Road.

5	Turn left on Jim Branch Trail at 1.3 miles. Begin a moderate climb, gaining 300 ft over the next 1.5 miles.
6	At 2.7 miles, turn right on Buck Forest Road.
7	Turn left on Thomas Cemetery Road at 2.9 miles.
8	At 3.0 miles pass Thomas Cemetery on your right. This small cemetery dates back to the 19th century; it's a great spot for photos and respectful exploring.
9	At 3.7 miles, turn right on Tarklin Branch Road.
10	At 4.2 miles, turn right on Wintergreen Falls Trail.
11	Arrive at Wintergreen Falls at 4.7 miles. This is the most secluded waterfall in DuPont State Forest. With caution, you can scramble over large boulders to different vantage points around the 20-ft falls.
12	Continue your hike by walking in the opposite direction on Wintergreen Falls Trail for 0.1 mile, then bear left on Sandy Trail at 4.8 miles.
13	After 400 ft on Sandy Trail, turn left on Grassy Creek Trail. This marks the start of the longest climb of the entire hike, which gains 400 ft over nearly 1.3 miles—but it is never strenuous.
14	At 5.7 miles, turn right on Joanna Road and continue to climb for 0.4 mile. Walk on Joanna Road for a total of 2.7 miles.
	Early bailout option Continue straight on Joanna Road for another 600 ft and turn right on Conservation Road. Walk 0.4 mile, turn left on Buck Forest Road, and follow route directions from #31 to reduce your total hiking distance to 10.3 miles.
15	At 8.4 miles, turn left on Pitch Pine Trail.
16	Arrive at Lake Dense at 8.6 miles. There's a covered picnic area and dock on the northwest side of the lake, a great place for lunch or a rest.
17	Continue around Lake Dense, and at 8.7 miles turn left on Three Lakes Trail, which re-enters the woods beyond the lake.
18	At a little past 9.1 miles reach the tiny 100-ft-wide Lake Alford. There's a short trail to the lake and a small dock with a bench.
19	After Lake Alford, turn left at the trail sign to continue your hike on Three Lakes Trail.
20	At 9.2 miles reach Lake Julia, at 99 acres the largest lake in DuPont State Forest.
21	At 9.4 miles, turn left on Conservation Road.

22	Turn right on Bridal Veil Falls Road at 9.8 miles.
23	Continue on Bridal Veil Falls Road for approximately 0.5 mile, ending at Bridal Veil Falls.
24	Return to Conservation Road and turn left.
25	At 12.0 miles bear right on Buck Forest Road.
26	Turn left on Lake Imaging Road at 12.6 miles. Immediately begin moderate ascent.
27	Walk 300 ft and turn left on Grassy Creek Falls Trail.
28	Continue another 650 ft on the trail to Grassy Creek Falls at 12.8 miles. **Caution** The last 200 ft descends uneven rocks and the top of the falls can be slippery.
29	Continue your hike by walking in the opposite direction on Grassy Creek Falls Trail. Turn right on Lake Imaging Road.
30	At 13.0 miles turn right on Buck Forest Road.
31	At 13.6 miles, continue on Buck Forest Road by bearing right and walking over the covered bridge, with beautiful views of Little River above High Falls.
32	Beyond the covered bridge at 13.7 miles, turn right on Covered Bridge Trail.
33	At 13.9 miles, turn right on High Falls Trail.
34	Begin descending into the High Falls area. You will begin to hear High Falls off to your right. After 300 ft, High Falls Trail makes a hard right and descends steeply for the next 0.1 mile.
35	At 14.2 miles come to split-rail fence to your right. This is the viewing and picture spot for High Falls.
36	Continue walking down High Falls Trail. At 14.6 miles bear right on Triple Falls Trail.
37	Walk 300 ft and the best views of Triple Falls come into view. To the right are wooden stairs leading to the bottom of the falls.
38	Continue down High Falls Trail. At 15.0 miles the trail goes under Staton Road and then crosses Little River Bridge.
39	At the end of the bridge, turn left on Hooker Falls Road.
40	At 15.3 miles reach Hooker Falls overlook and viewing platform. The trail descends steeply for 300 ft, reaching the river level.
41	Turn left at bottom of hill for the best views of Hooker Falls at 15.4 miles.

| 42 | Continue by walking in the opposite direction on Hooker Falls Road, and at 15.8 miles reach the parking area where you began. |

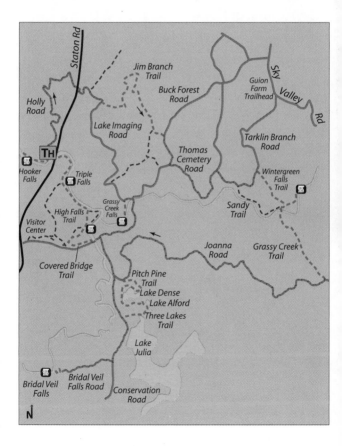

Hanging out at the base of Bridal Veil Falls.

DuPont State Forest

Mountain Bike Routes

Hikes that are Great Bike Rides

Bike nearly anywhere in DuPont

There are only two specific places in DuPont where biking is not allowed, and both are paths leading from parking areas: the white gravel trail from the High Falls/Visitor Center parking area and the trail section between the pedestrian bridge and Triple Falls leaving from the Hooker Falls trailhead parking area. In general, biking is also prohibited near waterfalls, protected habitats, and dangerous areas.

Routes for bikes

Starting on p. 86 are five rides that represent some of the best mountain biking in DuPont. These are routes not typically used by hikers.

Hike routes also recommended for biking

Short descriptions of these are listed below. See individual hike descriptions for maps and directions.

Jim Creek p. 34

A short ride that makes a nice addition to *Stone Mountain Loop* (p. 72).

Plantation Trail p. 42

Another short ride, it also makes a nice addition to *Stone Mountain Loop* (p. 72).

Grassy Creek Falls p. 44

An easy ride. You'll ride over the covered bridge across the top of High Falls. Grassy Creek Falls makes for a nice destination; just park your bike at the beginning of Grassy Creek Falls Trail and it's a very short walk down to the falls.

Wintergreen Falls p. 46

A fun destination on a mountain bike. It's mostly downhill to the falls and the climb back up is not too difficult. Park your bike near the horse tie-up and walk the last 100 ft or so to the falls.

Just pick a route; they're all good.

Three Lakes p. 48
A short ride with a big payoff. Allow plenty of time to hang out at the docks on Lake Dense or Lake Alford. You might even want to go for a swim.

Thomas Cemetery p. 50
An excellent beginner ride. You'll be riding on fairly level gravel roads for the entire route.

Bridal Veil Falls *via Conservation Road* p. 52
The absolute best and easiest way to get out and see Bridal Veil Falls. Riding a bike there is so much quicker than walking.

Bridal Veil Falls *via Corn Mill Shoals* p. 54
A great ride with some challenging climbs on bare rock. Add *Burnt Mountain* (p. 58) and/or *Cedar Rock* (p. 60) for an all-out ride.

Riding the "rock" of Cedar Rock Trail.

Burnt Mountain p. 58
This is a really fun loop to ride with some big whoops and a technical rock garden descent. Be sure to ride the loop in the opposite direction as is described in the hike directions and consider adding *Cedar Rock* (p. 60) for a longer loop.

Cedar Rock p. 60
Ride this route as described as a stand alone loop or add to any other route leaving from the same trailhead. Cedar Rock is where you'll encounter the most of DuPont's famous bare rock riding.

Lake Julia via Reasonover Creek Trail p. 62
You'll love this ride. There's a creek crossing, a big hill climb, a fast and crazy descent, and then a wind-out alongside a beautiful lake. Add this to *Mine Mountain* (p. 70) for a great double loop.

Sheep Mountain p. 64
The trails of this loop are one of DuPont's best kept mountain biking secrets. Cascade Trail, Pine Tree Trail, and Sheep Mountain are a hoot!

Hickory Mountain p. 66
Reverse the direction of the hike for a really fun bike loop, although you might want to keep the direction of Hickory Mountain Loop trail the same.

The Outer Limits p. 68
Ride this as an out-and-back or make a lollipop loop by riding Longside and Twixt trails to Rock Quarry Road to form the first half of the loop.

Mine Mountain p. 70
This is a great figure-8-style loop. It's awesome as is, but consider adding a side trip over to Bridal Veil Falls or combine it with *Lake Julia* (p. 62).

Stone Mountain p. 72
Yet another mountain biking secret of DuPont. The ride down from Stone Mountain is amazing. Be sure to ride opposite the direction specified in the described route.

23

Bike Primer Loop

Cyclists along Locust Trail.

Distance	6.7-mile loop
Difficulty	Easy
Location	Central DuPont, off Staton Road
Time	1.5 hours
Crowds	Light
Trailhead	Lake Imaging

Route Directions	
1	Begin on gravel Lake Imaging Road on the north side of the parking area.
2	At 0.3 mile begin a moderate climb that lasts nearly a mile.
3	Turn right on Hilltop Trail at 1.2 miles to begin singletrack.
4	Begin a short downhill at 1.5, descending into Grassy Creek Falls area.
5	At 2.1, turn right on Grassy Creek Falls Trail. Continue 200 ft, dismount, and walk your bike another 200 ft to top of Grassy Creek Falls, a great place to relax and check out the views.
6	Continue in the opposite direction on Grassy Creek Falls Trail.

7	At 2.4 miles, turn left on Lake Imaging Road and begin a moderate, 0.4-mile climb.
8	Turn right on Locust Trail at 2.6 miles. Begin singletrack and continue climbing.
9	At 3.0 miles, turn left on Isaac Heath Trail.
10	At 3.3 miles, turn right on Jim Branch Trail.
11	Turn left on gravel Buck Forest Road at 3.4 miles.
12	At 4.1 miles, turn left on White Pine Road.
13	Turn left on Hooker Creek Trail at 4.4 miles. This begins singletrack again, and 0.6 mile of fun downhill.
14	At 5.1 miles, begin a moderate, 0.5-mile climb.
15	At 5.5 miles, turn left on Ridgeline Trail. This is what you've been waiting for! Just past the start of this trail, you'll begin an awesome 1.1-mile singletrack downhill. Check your speed here; hikers frequent this trail.
16	At 6.5 miles turn right on gravel Lake Imaging Road.
17	Arrive at the parking area where you started your ride at 6.7 miles.

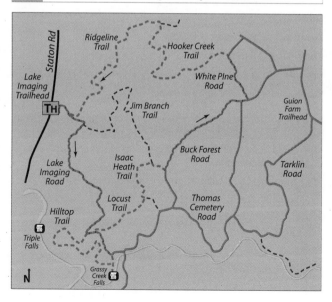

24

DuPont Bike Classic

Rest break at Lake Dense.

Distance	18.1-mile loop
Difficulty	Moderate
Location	Covers most of DuPont
Time	2.5 to 3.5 hours
Crowds	Light
Trailhead	High Falls/Visitor Center

	Route Directions
1	Begin at the end of the parking lot by going around the gate and riding down gravel Buck Forest Road.
2	Reach the covered bridge and turn right on gravel Conservation Road at 0.7 mile.
3	Continue on Conservation Road for 400 ft and turn sharply left on singletrack Pitch Pine Trail. This trail immediately begins a 0.2-mile climb, gaining over 100 ft.
4	At 1.1 miles cross Joanna Road, continuing on Pitch Pine Trail, which begins a descent to Lake Dense.

5	At 1.3 miles, arrive at Lake Dense.
6	Continue around the lake. At 1.5 miles turn left on Three Lakes Trail, which re-enters the woods at 1.6 miles.
7	Reach the 100-ft-wide Lake Alford at 1.8 miles. There's a short trail that leads to the lake and a small dock with a bench.
8	After visiting the lake, continue your ride on Three Lakes Trail.
9	At 2.0 miles arrive at 99-acre Lake Julia, DuPont State Forest's largest.
10	At 2.2 miles, turn left on gravel Conservation Road.
11	Begin a steep climb at 2.6 miles, gaining 230 ft over the next 0.5 mile. At the top of the hill, begin paralleling Airstrip Road to your right.
12	Continue straight on Shortcut Trail at 3.3 miles.
13	At bottom of steep hill, bear right on Conservation Road at 3.5 miles.
14	At 4.0 miles turn left on Reasonover Creek Trail. This fun singletrack immediately begins a steep descent into Reasonover Creek valley.
15	Cross Reasonover Creek at 4.3 miles and begin a sometimes steep 0.7-mile climb, gaining over 260 ft.
16	Turn right on Turkey Knob Road at 5.2 miles.
17	At 6.9 miles, turn left on Turkey Knob Trail.
18	At 7.1 miles, begin an exciting singletrack downhill lasting nearly 1.1 miles, losing 360 ft in elevation as you descend into the Briery Fork Creek valley.
19	Turn right on Briery Fork Trail at 8.0 miles.
20	At 8.4 miles, cross Joanna Road and continue straight to Grassy Creek Trail.
21	By 8.5 miles, begin another fun singletrack downhill lasting 0.7 mile, losing 250 ft in elevation as you descend into the Grassy Creek/Wintergreen valley.
22	Turn right on Sandy Trail at 9.3 miles. After 400 ft bear right on Wintergreen Falls Trail.
23	At 9.6 miles, arrive at Wintergreen Falls, the most secluded waterfall in DuPont and perfect for a mid-ride break.
24	Continue your ride by heading in the opposite direction on Wintergreen Falls Trail for 0.1 mile, then bear right, continuing on Wintergreen Falls Trail.
25	At 10.0 miles, turn right on Tarklin Branch Road and begin an easy 0.5-mile climb out of the valley.

Whooping it up on the banked turns of Ridgeline Trail.

26	Continue through a grassy field at 11.0 miles, passing Guion Farm parking area on your right.
27	At 11.3 miles, come to Buck Forest Road and almost immediately turn right on Hickory Mountain Road.
28	Turn left on Ridgeline Trail at 12.2 miles. By 12.4 miles, begin an awesome, 1.1-mile singletrack downhill. **Caution** Check your speed; hikers frequent this trail.
29	At 13.5 miles, turn left on Lake Imaging Road.
30	Ride 600 ft and turn left on Jim Branch Trail. This singletrack stretch climbs for nearly 0.8 mile, gaining over 200 ft.
31	At 14.8 miles, turn right on Isaac Heath Trail.
32	Continue straight across Lake Imaging Road to Hilltop Trail at 15.5 miles.
33	At 16.1, turn right on Grassy Creek Falls Trail. Bike 200 ft, dismount, and walk your bike another 200 ft to the top of Grassy Creek Falls. This is a great place to relax and check out the views.
34	Continue by reversing direction on Grassy Creek Falls Trail.
35	At 16.4 miles, turn right on Lake Imaging Road.

| 36 | At 16.5 miles, turn right on Buck Forest Road. |
| 37 | Continue on Buck Forest Road for 1.6 miles, ending your ride at the High Falls/ Visitor Center parking area where you began. |

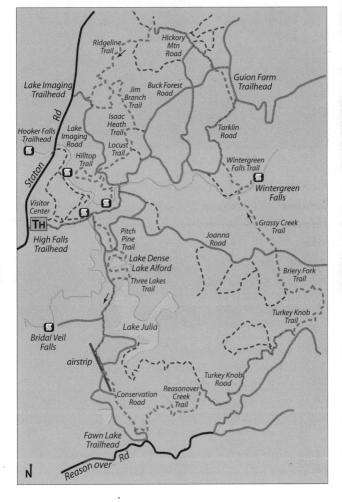

Big Day Mountain Bike

It's a long day on the Big Day Mountain Ride.

Distance	33.3-mile loop
Difficulty	Very strenuous
Location	Covers all of DuPont
Time	5 to 7 hours
Crowds	Moderate
Trailhead	Corn Mill Shoals

	Route Directions
1	Begin by crossing Cascade Lake Road, a wide trail with signage for Corn Mill Shoals Road/Cascade Lake Road.
2	After 150 ft, ride around gate. At intersection with Longside Trail continue straight; trail curves slightly to the right.
3	At 0.7 mile, come to first intersection with Burnt Mountain Trail. Continue straight, trail curves slightly to the right.
4	Turn right at second intersection with Burnt Mountain Trail.
5	Trail begins climbing at 1.6 miles and continues for 0.7 mile, gaining over 230 ft.

6	At 2.3 miles, begin a nearly 1-mile descent to bottom of Little Creek valley.
7	Turn right on Corn Mill Shoals Trail at 3.2 miles. Almost immediately, bear left on Little River Trail.
8	Continue past the first intersection with Cedar Rock Trail at 3.7 miles.
9	By 4.3 miles the route begins climbing, sometimes steeply, gaining nearly 400 ft over the next mile.
10	At 4.4 miles, turn left at the second intersection with Cedar Rock Trail.
11	Turn right on Big Rock Trail at 5.2 miles.
12	Begin rocky and sometimes technical 0.6-mile downhill.
13	At 6.0 miles turn left on Corn Mill Shoals Trail.
14	Arrive at the Little River at 7.1 miles. **Stop, evaluate water level and speed, and cross the river with caution.** Look directly across the creek to rocks where the trail continues. Removing your shoes and crossing the river in socks only provides the best traction; rocks in the riverbed are very slick.
15	After the crossing the trail becomes narrow singletrack. Turn right on Shoals Trail at 7.2 miles.
16	At 7.3 miles begin moderate climb 0.7-mile climb, gaining over 215 ft.
17	Turn right on Laurel Ridge Trail at 7.8 miles.
18	By 8.0 miles begin easy descent into Fawn Lake/Airstrip valley. This descent, with only a couple of flat stretches, lasts for nearly 1.6 miles.
19	At 8.3 miles turn left on Mine Mountain Trail.
20	Merge onto Fawn Lake Road at 8.4 miles.
21	Turn left on gravel Conservation Road at 8.6 miles.
22	Merge onto asphalt Airstrip Trail at 8.7 miles and continue on asphalt for 0.3 mile.
23	Turn left on singletrack Airstrip Trail at 9.0 miles.
24	At 9.8 miles turn left on Shelter Rock Trail.
25	At 10.0 miles, turn right on Corn Mill Shoals. Begin descent into Bridal Veil Falls valley; you'll begin to hear the falls within 0.2 mile.
26	Turn left on Bridal Veil Falls Road at 10.4 miles and visit the beautiful waterfall.
27	Continue the ride by reversing direction on gravel Bridal Veil Falls Road.

28	At 11.1 miles turn right on gravel Conservation Road.
29	At 11.3 miles, turn left on gravel Lake Julia Road and begin easy descent.
30	Turn right on Reasonover Creek Trail. At 11.7 miles turn right on Lake Julia Trail.
31	At 11.9 miles, arrive at rock crossing of Reasonover Creek. Dismount and walk your bike across the creek. You'll then climb for the next 1.4 miles, gaining over 360 ft.
32	Turn left on Turkey Knob Road at 13.3 miles.
33	At 15.0 miles, turn left on Turkey Knob Trail.
34	At 15.2 miles, begin a mile-long singletrack descent, losing the previous 360-ft gain as you descend into the Briery Fork Creek valley.
35	Turn right on Briery Fork Trail at 16.1 miles.
36	At 16.5 miles, come to Joanna Road. Continue straight across the road to Grassy Creek Trail.
37	By 16.6 miles, begin another fun singletrack downhill lasting 0.7 mile, losing 250 ft elevation as you descend into the Grassy Creek/Wintergreen valley.
38	Turn right on Sandy Trail at 17.4 miles. After 400 ft bear right on Wintergreen Falls Trail.
39	At 17.7 miles arrive at Wintergreen Falls, the most secluded waterfall in DuPont and a great place for a mid-ride break.
40	Continue by heading in the opposite direction on Wintergreen Falls Trail for 0.1 mile and then bear right, continuing on Wintergreen Falls Trail.
41	At 18.1 miles, turn right on Tarklin Branch Road and begin an easy 0.5- mile climb out of the valley.
42	Continue through a grassy field at 19.1 miles, passing Guion Farm parking area on your right.
43	At 19.4 miles come to Buck Forest Road; almost immediately turn right onto Hickory Mountain Road.
44	Turn left on Ridgeline Trail at 20.4 miles. By 20.6 miles trail begins a 1.1-mile singletrack downhill. **Caution** Check your speed; hikers frequent this trail.
45	At 21.8 miles, turn left on Lake Imaging Road.
46	Ride 600 ft. and turn left on Jim Branch Trail. This singletrack trail climbs for nearly 0.8 mile, gaining over 200 ft.
47	At 22.9 miles, turn right on Isaac Heath Trail.

48	Cross Lake Imaging Road at 23.6 miles and continue straight to Hilltop Trail.
49	At 24.6, turn right on Grassy Creek Falls Trail. Ride 200 ft, dismount ,and walk another 200 ft to the top of Grassy Creek Falls, a great place to relax and check out the views.
50	Continue by reversing direction on Grassy Creek Falls Trail.
51	At 24.8 miles, turn right on Lake Imaging Road.
52	At 24.9 miles, turn right on Buck Forest Road.
53	Continue to High Falls/Visitor Center parking area.
54	Pass through the parking area and turn right on Staton Road.
55	Ride 350 ft on Staton Road and turn left at the Sheep Mountain trailhead. Sheep Mountain Trail immediately begins a mile-long, moderate climb through a hardwood forest, gaining 240 ft.
56	At 28.0 miles, turn right on Cascade Trail.
57	Turn left on Pine Tree Trail at 29.0 miles.
58	Cross Staton Road at 29.3 miles, continuing on Pine Tree Trail.
59	At 29.5 miles, turn right on Longside Trail.
60	Turn right on Twixt Trail at 29.9 miles.
61	Cross Cascade Lake Road at 30.3 miles and begin gravel Rock Quarry Road. This begins the 1.3-mile final climb, gaining nearly 300 ft.
62	At 31.2 miles, turn left on Buck Ridge Road. After 500 ft, begin the descent to Corn Mill Shoals area; the rest of the ride is downhill or flat.
63	At the end of Buck Ridge Road, turn left on Micajah Trail.
64	Turn right on Wilkie Trail at 32.7 miles.
65	Arrive at Cascade Lake Road and continue to Corn Mill Shoals parking area to finish the ride at 33.3 miles.

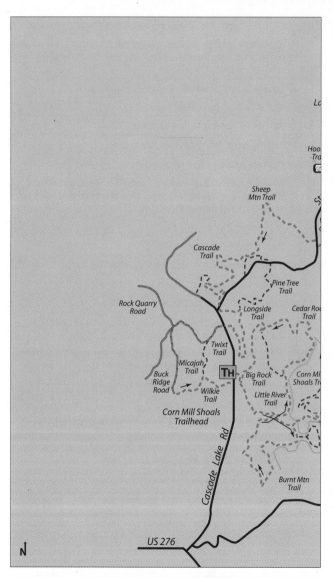

Lc

Hoo
Tra

Sheep
Mtn Trail

Cascade
Trail

Pine Tree
Trail

Rock Quarry
Road

Longside
Trail

Cedar Roc
Trail

Twixt
Trail

Micajah
Trail

TH

Big Rock
Trail

Corn Mi
Shoals Tr

Buck
Ridge
Road

Wilkie
Trail

Little River
Trail

Corn Mill Shoals
Trailhead

Burnt Mtn
Trail

Cascade Lake Rd

N

US 276

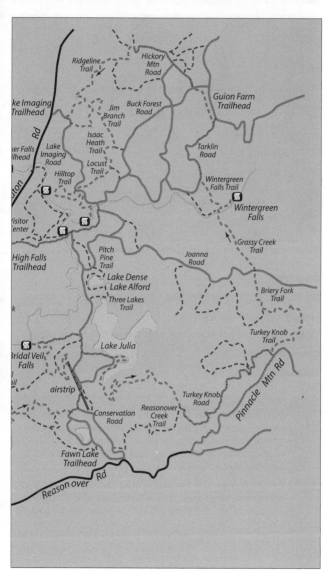

26

Kids Bike Loop

Raised boardwalks are just one of the challenges.

Distance	1+ mile
Difficulty	Easy, with some sharp turns on the boardwalk loops
Location	Northeast DuPont
Time	As little or as much time as you need to have a blast!
Crowds	Almost none
Trailhead	Guion Farm

Route Directions

The loop is just over a mile long and easy to follow in either direction. Look for the Kids Loop sign across from the northwest corner of the trailhead parking lot. From the entrance, ride to the right approximately 200 ft and the first skill area with a raised boardwalk is on the left.

The highlight of the loop is two skill areas. These offer a low-risk challenge to new mountain bikers. Continue another 150 ft down the trail to the second skill area on the left, offering more raised boardwalk loops, stability planks, and a teeter-totter.

A boardwalk and obstacles for bikers of all ages

Despite its official name, it's a great place for mountain bikers of all ages to practice stability and agility. However, if there are kids in the skills area and you're not one, be patient and wait until they're finished before giving the obstacles a try.

Caution The boardwalks and other wooden skill areas are very slippery when wet, even with morning dew.

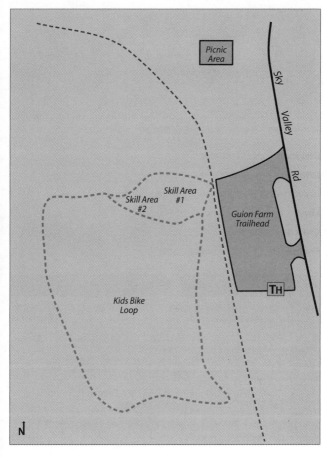

27

Gravel Mixer

Gravel Buck Forest Road is easy to navigate.

Distance	16.1-mile loop
Difficulty	Moderate
Location	Covers the eastern limits of DuPont
Time	1.5 to 2.5 hours
Crowds	Light
Trailhead	High Falls/Visitor Center

	Route Directions
1	Begin at the end of the parking lot by going around the gate and riding down gravel Buck Forest Road.
2	Reach the covered bridge and continue straight on Buck Forest Road (by bearing slightly to the left) at 0.7 miles.
3	At 1.1 miles after crossing bridge, bear right to continue on Buck Forest Road.
4	Turn right on gravel Sky Valley Road at 3.0 miles. **Caution** Though traffic is typically light, this road is open to motor vehicles.
5	By 3.4 miles, Sky Valley Road begins a 0.6-mile climb, gaining over 275 ft; it is steep and rutted at times.

6	At 6.0 miles, turn right on Pinnacle Mountain Road. This old 4WD road is rutted with rocks and mud holes (which are easily avoided) and sees very little vehicle traffic. Despite a few small climbs you'll lose more than 700 ft over its 6 miles.
7	At 12.0 miles the gravel ends. Turn right on asphalt Reasonover Road.
8	Turn right on gravel Conservation Road at 12.8 miles. Ride around the gate and continue straight.
9	At 13.4 miles, bear right on gravel Shortcut Trail, continuing steeply uphill.
10	Continue straight, rejoining Conservation Road at 13.8 miles.
11	At 14.4 miles, pass Lake Julia.
12	Continue on Conservation Road for 1.0 mile and turn left on Buck Forest Road (at covered bridge) at 15.4 miles.
13	Ride 0.7 mile on Buck Forest Road, ending your ride where you began.

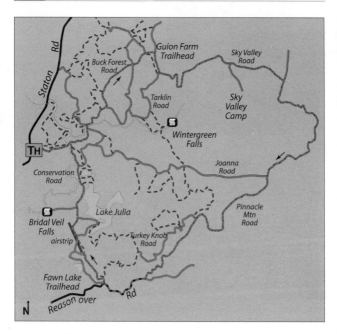

Parts of the DuPont woods are filled with green ferns.

Appendices

Appendix A: Routes by Trailhead

High Falls/Visitor Center

Hooker Falls

Lake Imaging

Guion Farm

Corn Mill Shoals

Fawn Lake

Routes with Ancillary Trailheads

Appendix B: Management Resources

DuPont State Recreational Forest
PO Box 300
Cedar Mountain, NC 28718
828-877-6527
ncforestservice.gov

Friends of DuPont Forest
dupontforest.com

Emergency Phone Numbers

North Carolina Forest Service	800-727-5928
Henderson County Emergency	828-697-4596
Transylvania County Emergency	828-884-3168
Or dial 911	

Appendix C: Local Outfitters & Bike Shops

WNC Outfitters

Asheville

Black Dome Mountain Sports
140 Tunnel Road
Asheville, NC 28805
828-251-2001
blackdome.com

Blackrock Outdoor Company
570 W Main St
Sylva, NC 28779
828-631-4453
blackrockoutdoorcompany.com

Diamond Brand Outdoors
1378 Hendersonville Rd
Asheville, NC 28803
828-684-6262
53 Biltmore Ave
Asheville, NC 28801
828-771-4761
diamondbrand.com

Frugal Backpacker
52 Westgate Pkwy
Asheville, NC 28806
828-209-1530
frugalbackpacker.com

REI Asheville
Biltmore Park Town Square
31 Schenck Pkwy
Asheville, NC 28803
828-687-0918
rei.com

WNC Bike Shops

Pisgah Forest

Sycamore Cycles
112 Hendersonville Hwy
Pisgah Forest, NC 28768
828-877-5790
sycamorecycles.com

The Hub
49 Pisgah Hwy #60
Pisgah Forest, NC 28768
828-884-8670
thehubpisgah.com

Asheville

Asheville Bicycle Company
1000 Merrimon Ave
Asheville, NC 28804
828-254-2771
ashevillebicyclecompany.com

Beer City Bicycles
144 Biltmore Ave
Asheville, NC 28801
828-575-2453
beercitybicycles.com

Billy Goat Bicycles
5 Regent Park Blvd # 106
Asheville, NC 28806
828-525-2460
billygoatbikes.com

Carolina Fatz
1240 Brevard Rd #3
Asheville, NC 28806
828-665-7744
carolinafatzmountainbicycle.com

Epic Cycles
800 Haywood Rd
Asheville, NC 28806
828-505-4455
epiccyclesnc.com

Hearn Cycling
28 Asheland Ave
Asheville, NC 28801
828-253-4800

Liberty Bicycles
1378 Hendersonville Rd
Asheville, NC 28803
828-274-2453
libertybikes.com

Motion Makers Bicycle Shop
878 Brevard Rd
Asheville, NC 28806
828-633-2227
motionmakers.com

Youngblood Bicycles
233 Merrimon Ave
Asheville, NC 28801
282-251-4686
youngbloodbikes.com

Hendersonville

Sycamore Cycles
146 3rd Ave
Hendersonville, NC 28792
828-693-1776
sycamorecycles.com

The Bicycle Company
779 N Church St #A
Hendersonville, NC 28792
828-969-1500
thebikecompany.com

Waynesville

Rolls Rite Bicycles
1362 Asheville Rd
Waynesville, NC 28786
828-276-6080
rollsritebicycles.com

Sylva

Motion Makers Bicycle Shop
36 Allen St
Sylva, NC 28779
828-586-6925
motionmakers.com

Bryson City

Bryson City Bicycles
157 Everett St
Bryson City, NC 28713
828-488-1988
brysoncitybicycles.com

Tsali Cycles
35 Slope St
Bryson City, NC 28713
828-488-9010
tsalicycles.com

Upstate South Carolina Outfitter & Bike Shops

Travelers Rest

Sunrift Adventures
1 Center St
Travelers Rest, SC 29690
864-834-3019
sunrift.com

Greenville

Appalachian Outfitters
191 Halton Rd
Greenville, SC 29607
864-987-0618
appoutfitters.com

Carolina Triathlon
928 S Main St
Greenville, SC 29601
864-331-8483
carolinatriathlon.com

Half-Moon Outfitters
1420 Laurens Rd
Greenville, SC 29607
864-233-4001
halfmoonoutfitters.com

REI Greenville
The Point
1140 Woodruff Rd #400
Greenville, SC 29607
864-297-0588
rei.com

Sunshine Cycle Shop
1826 N Pleasantburg Dr
Greenville, SC 29609
864-244-2925
sunshinecycle.com

Trek Bicycle Store of SC
1426 Laurens Rd
Greenville, SC 29607
864-235-8320
trekbikessouthcarolina.com

TTR Bikes
101 S Hudson St
Greenville, SC 29601
864-283-6401
ttrbikes.com

Spartanburg

Bike Worx
1321 Union St
Spartanburg, SC 29302
864-542-2453
bikeworx.net

The Local Hiker
173 E Main St
Spartanburg, SC 29306
864-764-1651
thelocalhiker.com

Trek Bicycle Store of SC
105 Franklin Ave
Spartanburg, SC 29301
864-574-5273
trekbikessouthcarolina.com

Pickens

Southern Appalachian Outdoors
506 W Main St
Pickens, SC 29671
864-507-2195

Clemson

Elkmont Trading Company
100 Liberty Dr
Clemson, SC 29631
864-653-7002
elkmonttradingcompany.com

Anderson

Grady's Great Outdoors
3440 Clemson Blvd
Anderson, SC 29621
864-226-5283
gradysoutdoors.com

Trek Bicycle Store of SC
2714 N Main St
Anderson, SC 29621
864-226-4579
trekbikessouthcarolina.com

About the Author

Scott Lynch has been hiking and mountain biking along the trails of the Carolinas since 1989. A business and technical writer who is also the author of *Family Hikes in Upstate South Carolina* and *Hiking South Carolina's Foothills Trail*, he lives in the South Carolina Upstate.

Notes

Notes

Milestone Press

Hiking

- *Backpacking Overnights:
  NC Mountains, SC Upstate*
  by Jim Parham

- *Day Hiking the
  North Georgia Mountains*
  by Jim Parham

- *Hiking Atlanta's
  Hidden Forests*
  by Jonah McDonald

- *Hiking North Carolina's
  Blue Ridge Mountains*
  by Danny Bernstein

- *Hiking the
  Carolina Mountains*
  by Danny Bernstein

- *Family Hikes in
  Upstate South Carolina*
  by Scott Lynch

- *Waterfalls Hikes of
  North Georgia*
  by Jim Parham

- *Waterfalls Hikes of
  Upstate South Carolina*
  by Thomas E. King

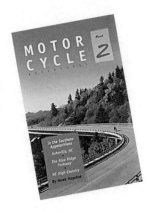

Motorcycle Adventure Series
by Hawk Hagebak

- *1–Southern Appalachians:
  North GA, East TN,
  Western NC*

- *2–Southern Appalachians:
  Asheville NC,
  Blue Ridge Parkway,
  NC High Country*

- *3–Central Appalachians:
  Virginia's Blue Ridge,
  Shenandoah Valley,
  West Virginia Highlands*

Mountain Bike Guides
by Jim Parham

- *Mountain Bike Trails—
  NC Mountains &
  SC Upstate*
- *Mountain Bike Trails—
  North GA &
  Southeast TN*

Milestone Press

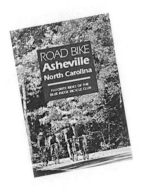

Road Bike Guide Series

- *Road Bike Asheville, NC* by the Blue Ridge Bicycle Club

- *Road Bike North Georgia* by Jim Parham

- *Road Bike the Smokies* by Jim Parham

Family Adventure

- *Natural Adventures in the Mountains of North Georgia* by Jim Parham & Mary Ellen Hammond

Pocket Guides

- *Hiking South Carolina's
  Foothills Trail*
  by Scott Lynch
- *Hiking & Mountain Biking
  DuPont State Forest*
  by Scott Lynch
- *Hiking & Mountain Biking
  Pisgah Forest*
  by Jim Parham

Can't find the Milestone Press guidebook you want at a
bookseller near you? Call us at 828-488-6601 or visit
milestonepress.com for purchase information.